glitter

bath

by addie wuensch

a free spirited book of poetry

and prose

$*&@!#?<=%

dedicated to my grandmother lola walker!

Art Vortex with Ashes

The flower began to slump over

The stem began to break

Dressed in black and rain-soaked holding this broken white orchid

When she shut herself in to paint, her canvas, like a tiny graveyard

Mimicking an even smaller universe, opened up,

6 or more feet down and actualized as the equivalent of a portal to

somewhere in space

Like a vortex of toys and teeth

A blur of a few birthdays and Christmases

She painted the ashes

Into her piece that sat reverent like a Bible on its stand

And the paint swallowed the matter like an ocean settling and calming

sand onto its bottom

She manifested her intentions

For her child into her art

Created, as a mantra for healing, a vice, and a cross to clutch

The body was broken and given like last communion

Burnt and condensed by the elements into its original form

Materialized from stardust

A spiritual flesh-vessel sacrifice to the art-God

Given to an audience who cannot understand

A place of rest, hope-more than a source of texture

A painting that can never be finished-a physical burden that can never

be discarded

Pressure to make beauty in death, something that cannot be

paralleled

By earthly aesthetics

++++Metaphorical Universe

Beds of wet moss call out to tiny fingers like pillowtop mattresses to tired bodies. I fall on my hands and bruised knees and I soak my pants and most of my shirt in the flowing water that passes through the shifting rocks and through my growing soul like liquid light through frosted broken glass. This water passes over me as I let myself sink into the depth of this creek, as I become part of this cycle that is inside me, and everyone, giving and taking, keeping us alive. My hands grip whatever lines the bottom, and fingertips sink into silt and are buried like treasure.

Tiny earthy memoirs collect in my palms and slip into my little pockets like wet ideas. Sparkling beauties in the sun, a poor child's pirate find, worth more than the pennies and nickels clinking next to the newly found stones. The earth opens up to my tiny feet, and acknowledges my existence on its surface. I felt the truth of the art that was a wordless wonder. The words that were written on the earth with dust and fish and quartz sang prose that told me art was survival. Art was food and water. The earth was art. The earth, in harmony with art was hope for hopeless manic artists everywhere. Imagination and reality marry to channel another dimension. 3d and 2d and nonverbal and musical reads the earth like a staff..... and those who are different *step with footsteps that shock like graffiti on its crust*

I feel as if too many people in New York take themselves entirely too seriously. My IQ drops exponentially when I ride the G train. I can't stop eyeing everyone and almost bursting into a hysterical fit of church giggles when I ride the train because everyone plays the "i-wont-look-at-you-but-if-i-do-you-wont-catch-me-looking-at-you-but-if-you-catch-me-or-if-i-catch-you-looking-it-will-just-be-extremely-awkward-game." Everyone looks so solemn as if we are currently attending the Pope's funeral. When I see these people and their seriousness, I just want to yell out something spectacular. Burst into song. Throw out some jazz hands.

$$$

New York amazes me. I have felt peace in New York in the most chaotic. A crowded subway car with all colors and classes and intentions and cultures and backgrounds and destinations with voices layering and droning to a beautiful hum. We are one. I feel peace while walking through Times Square every day on the way to and from the designer I am doing a month long in-house job for's studio. I can't wait to feel the rush of cars and smoke and smells and love where everyone crosses and exchanges with creative human intensity. It's a treat, every moment of it. A treat that I can have, unlike the hotdogs or candied nuts in the stands.

$$$

I am so humbled by the talent here. Singers sing, dancers dance, painters paint, mimers mime-performance artists do strange things on the subway-in the stations-on the street-wherever they feel inspired to create and perform they do it-with such beautiful passion and talent and these people are so complexly talented. Genius versus madness is a constant battle-slash-broadway-sidewalk-show. Some seem broken, and some seem thankful to be blessed with a gift no matter how humble their stage is.

The energy here is unreal. I want to stay here as long as I can. A piece of my soul has been given as a sacrificial investment that almost parallels spiritual worship that is the equivalent of my becoming a part of this motherearthcitythatsalivingbreathingbeingwithheartLungsandabrainand feelingsandexcrements as the energy is the blood that flows though this city being's veins and we are the cells, white and red, fighting and regenerating and innovating and healing and mutating and evolving and living and dying.

$$$

A homeless man named Kelly lives in my yard. When I use the word "yard" I am referring to the random slab of concrete that is next to my Brooklyn brownstone. He screams, and yells, and drags massive pieces of metal things such as old stoves or radio wires and strews them in front of our apartment and down the block, tearing them apart. It's beautiful. He collects old windows then smashes them in front of my apartment. This guy must be an artist. I believe this guy is an installation artist. He sings to us, sometimes we feed him, and once he told us he was our guardian angel.

$$

Every day it takes an hour to get to where I need to go in the city. At every casting, there are so many models that have outstandingly unique and beautiful outsides. Initially, I believed that ultimately inner beauty would show though and conquer and that because "I'm a good person" my positive energy would prevail. What a self-indulgent, bullshit ideal. I have slowly began to realize that my childlike, naive and romanticized views of what the world is like and should be like are not quite always accurate. While some people in the world, the people I seek, may have wisdom to share and be philosopher kings with awareness and understanding and a desire for peace and unity, I am not likely to find many of these philosopher kings in the modeling industry. But I will find them in the city...I am on a quest......

$$$

My 15 year old roommate got raped. We were in the emergency room for 12 hours. This hospital is like a third world country. I feel like a mother. I feel like a grown-up.

$$$

Sadly, my coked out roommate, the star of the agency who books all the jobs and treats everyone like shit, especially me, ODed on the couch. I took care of her and another girl called 911. She continued to treat me like shit even after this.

$$$

Eventually she gets off drugs and apologizes. I admire her courage to do so. I think she may be experiencing some clarity. I forgive her. Who am I to judge her? I'm not perfect. No one is perfect.

$$$

I met someone, he changed my life. Platonic friendship but maybe a soul mate...........he treats me like a person and reminds me that my ideals are not contrived and that is okay to simply be myself and be a free spirit no matter the constraints of the industry and that some people are not yet jaded and its okay to see the world as beautiful and hopeful...................he is beauty. He is hope. He is art.

$$$

This person who I met, François, musician/promoter/old soul, has taken me all around the city to do the most spectacular things anyone could ever experience. After this summer, what could possibly top this experience? Heaven was this Soho Indian Summer. Upper West Side. Bedsty. Collective..

$$$

I have discovered the Chelsea galleries. If this was a bottomless lake, I fell in and drowned in its artistic brilliance. I realize that I am an artist, and my path and purpose in New York is for inspiration and art of all mediums. I am meant to be here and create.

Odd Perspective - Revisited

Seven flowers, petals drenched in glue

A bed of glitter for its appendages

The petals roll, shine, stick, dry

Morning, collecting treasures

Pocket them, protected poison, expensive

Walk to your train, the C

Artist, collecting energy

The street performer platform

Feet planted softly on his ground

the man made earth he owns

street king, street queens

Reach in, pull out sparkling petals

Drop them into welcoming chakra

Feeding artist metaphors among coins

Like a carnival ride, artist lights up,

A crown of thorns made from organic and antique, faded Christmas

bulbs from the 50s

That radiate from scalp like tea lights

He is rich

In creation, form, movement

He merges

And train, seeing through two front lights, eyes that see blur, smoke

Flesh, sitting/standing/avoiding/watching

Exchanges

Slow/stop/fly/arrive

Housing us together for moments together in transitive purgatory

Inside shaking vessels moving sideways

Watching at a diagonal those who remain on the platform

As we are tossed into this tunnel of pollution and fate

(a Wedding Ring)

Buildings grow tall like new buds coming of age in sunlight

Quartz and Rainbow moonstone are harvested, murdered, preserved

Like a human sacrifice for a sturdy finger for rebirth

Stones with soul, waiting for earthy hands to embrace intention

Only in separation from darkness can the blind stone emanate light

like strings

To bring energy from the deep ground to surface cities and express

change

Exuberance-Madness and 1000 Volts of Electricity

Now we need Pepsi

To wash her American Blood

Off of the street where this

Overworked, lonely and drunken

Truck driver left her body-also alone

To die from the heavy wheels of his American loneliness and

carelessness

An epidemic, catalyzing

Addiction and death

The driver sips his cola, gagging on God

As his road kill lay, cheapened like circus waste,

Like a prize in his rearview for stuffing and mounting

Mutilated, dehumanized

Body un-beautified, bare for world when the sun rises and people will

scrape her remains from onlooker's sight

Organs dismembered and eaten by the light-speed pirouette,

her spirit free as a dance with 1000 pastel ribbons, from sunrise

straight to space—she waits for nothing, she is exuberance

Nature VS Nurture

He is so beautiful as he lay asleep in his 9 x 9 white bed with his open window behind him and the tops of the buildings behind him line his head like a crown of thorns. I wish I could stay here forever with him and let him be my ivy-league Jesus but I have things to do in North Carolina where I'm living and learning and growing into a woman alone in a place that sometimes seems, in comparison to my City, like a third world country.

I leave through his elevator-passageway and I am on to the streets where I'm feeling a different sort of city than I've felt before. I let myself feel. I feel the cityscapes that lined his walls that now live and grow upwards like hungry buds coming of age into plants beneath my feet and climbing above my head as I am 34 floors down from him and walking the cold streets of Manhattan. I am feeling so much as the thirsty plantlike buildings drink this freezing rain as I let it pelt my skin like tiny ideas that sting like punishment and for now we are alike. I let myself feel the millions of dreams and ideas that grip my arms and legs and face and organs with Technicolor hands capable like a surgeon's with sharp nails for cutlery that rip into me gently as I am pieced for the togetherness of the city. The city is my seamstress, stitching me up and tightening my strings as if I'm a corset, and all I can do is think and dream in metaphors and take this all in.

I let myself feel the cold. I took off my jacket and let myself feel cold on my face and hair as if I was housing a million tiny worlds inside complicated raindrops with beautiful landscapes and histories and intentions waiting to be explored by revolutionaries on primitive ships. I wanted these worlds to create a big bang and wash away this lie, this mask, this overpriced make-up from my face until I was bare on these streets in front of all of these blurred people passing, and I would be unnoticed as usual, another flesh-colored blur; a little more free.

I would see their faces and hope I was beautiful to myself underneath this shit I have caked all over myself like some kind of porcelain stripper. Underneath this makeup I am much more human and tainted; maybe more likable. Maybe more disgusting! Maybe wiser! Maybe happier.

The nature of these blocks that pass are to be multi-faceted with themes and colors and design and beautiful, diverse people. I inch towards the park and as the rain dries, I finally feel the park next to me, as I am in full speed with fast feet, and the park is full of children and wise old trees, full of life, full of joyful escape and primitive stories are constantly whispered as the people of this beautiful city scurry out from behind their hideouts like little animals after a storm.

I stood underneath the wet statues near the park at Columbus Circle and watched the corpses of rain drip generously off of the strength of the arms and body of the men towering over my tiny head that someone sculpted long ago. Birds are gathering on their bodies and their concrete muscles are crevices for the comfort of their tiny, humble feet. I experience nature and nurture depicted in my fleetingly photographic memory.

Nature. Nurture. Republicans. Democrats. Socialism. Anarchy. Art. Music. Film. Imagination. Sex. Death. Life. Abortion. Pain. Religion. Culture. Color. Sound. Dance. Math. Science. History. Astrology. Healing. Abstract. Reality. Purpose. God. Animals. Love. Feeling. God.

I leave my dreamlike state of walking poetry to join again the concrete waking life to gather up some presents for this sleeping man. I'm going to cook my famous spicy coconut curry for him tonight and I want to get some delicious ingredients. I meet up with my chosen

sister who inspires and encourages me beyond my comprehension. I

share with her my crazy thoughts and dreams and she seems to

understand. We obsess over everything wonderful in the gigantic

health food store of my dreams. Then, in and out of stores, I come

across a lonely white orchid. I purchase it and grab a cab back to his

place because the rain has started again.

I walked through the door of his beautiful white apartment where

everything was perfect except for me. He was upset that I was gone

for so long.

$$$

The flower began to slump over. The stem began to break. Dressed

all in black, and rain soaked, holding this broken white orchid.

%%

I'm leaving today- in an hour. He walked me through Lincoln Center where I could feel that he spent a lot of time. I could sense that it was important to him to share this place with me and for me to appreciate it, and his connection to it. Everything within this hour felt so meaningful.

His dark hair was wild. His metaphysical communicates with his physical and it comes out daily through his wiry hair that varies from day to day to reflect his moods. His hair fell across his little nose and some strands remained tucked beneath his earlobes. Right now he reminds me so much of my little brother, all grown up. They are brilliant material from the same star.

I realized, at Lincoln Center, I'm a grown up now. I have this boyfriend in a suit with a PHD. Even though-underneath his slacks and manshoes he is wearing snoopy socks there is a hint of seriousness to the situation. I'm a big girl. I have a flower in my hair and a poem in my heart. I'm almost 6 feet tall. I'm a woman.

I'm a big girl who is a

<<<<<* crazy ! artist of the abstract sort >>>>>

and he is a man who dreams in math and LOgic.

123456789. = He's a professoR

at Columbia teaching things I cannot begin to Understand while I write and pAint things that confUse hiM and **h**e writes it off

aS nonsense insteaD of realizing Everything i painT and Write in content and forM are Metaphors done with confiDence,

and there is a Meaning, puRpose, or ∎ mystery **?**

attAched with iNsinuated imaginative   formulas created by the

spirit. The RULES he lives by I break.

Our expressiveness

is not to be tainted

with constraints.

"These steps light up, you know." He pointed out. As I was feeling each long, concrete step underneath my combat boots, I pictured each one of them lighting up underneath my feet one by one, and I wondered if I could ever explain to him how much I understood and appreciated him. I care for him, and appreciate him, but he is not the one.

&&&&&&&&&&&&&&&&&&&&&&&&&&&&&&&&&&&&&&&&&&&&&&&&&

I see, with much more clarity that everything in the world is so beautiful and complicated and dark and light and I wish I could write it out, like graffiti on walls-each spoken sentence could been translated to poetry or art and I wouldn't be forced into my awkward verbal purgatory with people while my expression seems so contrived and my head and mouth don't match. I wish I could omit and erase whatever didn't fit and throw it out before it was expressed. I could just hold up a canvas with a picture and people would smile and nod. I could just snap photographs at the speed of light and hold them up and draw arrows and beep at them with morse code. This thought makes me laugh- that I suck at talking this much and that the city makes me feel this expressive and new.

I wish I could prolong time to take everything in, process it inside my heart and mind, laugh and cry intermittently with freedom and honesty and humanity. I wish gays and straights, races, religions, cultures, classes, ages-could come together to live in peace. I wish each human and animalistic interaction was a display of expressive artistic beauty and love. I wish I could hug everyone and tell them everything would be okay. And I wish someone would do the same for me. And during all of the extras—time would speed up to light speed where all of my intentions would be expressed so quickly that they would be understood like the blink of an eye, not long and drawn out like a story. People would just understand each other's insides. And everything would fall and dry like acrylic paint, fast and fixable-but this would be bittersweet-and ruin the mystery of the universe.

I'd like for him to understand my unreasonable desires that are accomplishable only on a silly metaphysical level and I'd attempt to speak to him in equations that id let him solve and praise him when he got them right.

Secrets+sex+stress — flowers x a little champagne x philosophy x spiritual connection and enlightenment / future husband – my loneliness + cobalt blue paint mixed with white + my needs + your needs – the truth about you – white canvas x fate x the mysterious and famous variable y = what? Show your work.

%%%%%%%%%%%%%%%%%%%%%%%%%%%%%%%%%%%%%%%

So eventually I gave him this equation. It was a much more diluted, less honest, raw and abstract version of the original equation, but mathematicians are used to that by now.

%%%%%%%%%%%%%%%%%%%%%%%%%%%%%%%%%%%%%%%

I am beyond inspired by the city and by new love. I can paint it to him and to the world through shapes and colors that mean the world to me, giving meaning to my symbolism hoping that if I throw in numbers like Stuart Davis, that he will get the hint.

In everything, this time, during my visit to my City, there is a sort of beautiful and notably differ philosophy that creates questions within questions and everything is a kinetic web that extends across the city's wide universe as we inch closer to each other. I am looking at myself differently. I feel more assertive. More confident in who I am and in my ability to create and be–my ability to feel, process, interpret. I am, as an individual, without any man, strong and actualizing. Any relationship from now on will just be a positive plus in addition to the life I am starting and the self-love I am working on and achieving. This is a milestone for me, for I have spent much time disliking and disrespecting myself. Each time I am in the city it is life changing. If I am single forever, I know the city will always be there, waiting to marry me.

$$

Understanding that I may not ever fully understand gives me a lot of peace. In the past I began to understand that everyone I had loved so far has saved me from the last one and prepared me for the next one.

$$

melodramatic muffin 11

awkward and bony with dangling shoelaces

wearing sunglasses to cover dark sockets

smirking behind closed door of

shiny elevator box

equipped like a hipster, beadies in buttoned shirt pocket

for organic, sneaky, sarcastic elevator smoke time

thats better than yours

beautiful sensory mixup

hears color and sees sound

tastes dirty words and tobacco

her halo is made of cynical oranges, grapefruits from the health food

store

her skin, acidic, citrus flavored cancer

she'll never die she'll just compost your garden

Crosshatching

Hatching, crosshatching, pencil, ink, minds, meshing

Connection is the sharing of pain

Money. Crosshatching. Smiles. Crosshatching

Middle East. Forests. Wildlife.

Exploration of boundaries that may or may not exist

They are growing together in colorful poetry like roots that wrap

around feet and ankles

Grounding, separating us

From strategic chasing of numbers

Materialized

The death of his planet

Means stardust is raining down

Like powdered sugar cane

As he is now grounded on her earth

They are coated in our day

As the gunshots are quieted by stomach ache sweet and nausea

Their showers have run dry and been replaced with holocaust traps

As the stench of chocolate coats our backs and they can't wash it

away with what's in this Pail

Dreams that Exhaust

He was alone

With himself

And his damaged spirit

Searching for a reason to sleep, to wake in dreaming from his waking

nightmares

Where she's half-alive, eyes bugged out-disturbed

Calling for him and he cannot reach her with words or touch

Vineyard

His vineyard was overgrown with grapes and soul

His late wife

Wandered barefoot with her wine

In the plush grass, her eyes light

Gaze, raised, over the soft hill, olive grand

Into the valley's seemingly tiny river the size of her raised index finger,

her feet stepping slowly towards the inviting water

As he watched her contentment

As if it were his greatest accomplishment

Waking life

Today, I don't notice that

I'm aching in this death trap corset

Even if I break a few ribs along the way

If my body is maimed and disfigured, will I be replaced by someone

younger, more beautiful, more willing and able for this machine?

Waking Life-Reflection/ 20-30

My reflections are literal mirrors of caves with whalebone discoveries

Hand-holding and liberation

Mapping evolution on each other's spines, tracing bones with hungry

fingers

Immense hips pair with ours for birthing as we are all creatures

speaking different languages

Producing, reproducing, feeling, loving, growing.

Waking Life- Moral

I'm in this extravagant kitchen, devouring shortbread

As I can feel myself ballooning into obesity

I am married, and just as his paintbrush

 Brushes softly over my welcoming body

My soul is sliding straight into hell.

Shadow of Beauty

Morning light falls like snow on my light forehead and shoulders,

breasts and thighs

I'm studying my flaws in the mirror like tiny taxidermy creatures under

glass

In this round, full mirror on its firm stand

It sits, like a person, waiting for a moving moment of radiance

As it absorbs the beauty it seeks, it will crack, and shatter, usable

only for tiny mice

Who collect the debris for their abodes

Fantasize

A swing as a catapult to the sky

The old woman becomes young again in the time travel seat to the

sky of masochistic

cures for cystic fibrosis with performance art deathbeds in galleries

for critique

And her shape has changed to a young, newborn rhombus with no

human attributes

As the shapes of the universe had just gone through labor and had

twins, birthing her, and someone else

As silent, crying, faceless shapes, clunking dully when they hit the

ground without an umbilical cord

Change Size

Before her death, her veins swell like giants for the needle,

Manning her body and growing heads, 2 heads,

That have thirsty tongues that lasso the needle and slurp the poison

from the prick.

Clouds come from the edge of the earth and draw blood to keep, with

sharp lightning, As her earth-body dries up, the clouds keep her cells

Transfer

She's at Mickey D's clogging her arteries

And contributing to a massive, worldwide brainwashing mechanism

For speed and ignorance. Cast in bronze for the Olympic treasure

Her face is immobile

And mounted on ribbons in the center of the winners' torsos

In Creation

Erosion and storms, filling it

Like a newborn's vein fills with blood, a canal for creatures, discovery,

and cleansing

Walls for the first graffiti I had ever seen-the first forts we had ever

built

It dreamed, branching out, drawing in more tiny bare feet and

handmade poles

Until huge boots came with machinery and dumped gravel into its

sides,

Weighing it down with man-made burden

Like the mind of an American in public K-12

Prevented from expansion

In Death

It craved and coveted lakes and oceans

Colorful treasures from the Corning dump,

Hungry for frosted glass boulders that were like nothing I had ever

seen

For gentle teeth made of water and fish

Promoting understanding of the environment

And the earth in harmony with dirty thoughtless people

Its openness was a cleansing site for spiritual growth

And it spent its retirement as a memory as only I attended its funeral.

Isolate

Her legs lay on separate planes of the planet

Her chest mounted on a chapel

Her toes scattered across a fast food parking lot

Her lipstick, like graffiti on stone, red as blood

Smeared and nonsensical on detached lips, blowing in cheap currents

Her fingers, gripping broken branches blowing across highways into

ditches

With welcoming cushions of water

She has never breathed, only broken, her machinery and wires were

Mass produced for the system and never put together properly

And the world is her grave

American Flag in Black White and Grey

(Ode to an Artist with ADHD Who Attempts to Fill a Void with a

Man)

 I.

There's a rain soaked grey FCUK

Sweatshirt hanging on the telephone wire

Near your neatly painted white garage apartment

Like an ornament of middle class mischief

I park my silver PT Cruiser

With my peace sign sticker

And 4 cheap hubcaps

By the street in front of

Your rich landlord's mansion

Because he has parked all of his cars in the spaces

So I'll have to walk

Up the dirt alley

To your self-proclaimed "slave quarters"

I'm saving up for therapy

Not an SUV

I'm a borderline self-sufficient artist seeking fellow artists

To bitch with

We can bitch about how non artists can suck our cock

And how we rule the world with our art from our little low rent

Apartments

Because we suck at making money but we think our ideas are fucking

Great

We are walking parity, hand me beret

##

She don't have health insurance

And she "ain't" seen a dime

Of Daddy's

money

II.

I'm fidgety and ADD, strange and full of ideas but no one gives a fuck

My cell phone is dead and my hands are texting pure air on autopilot

I'm writing poetry with no pen, with no machine

Visions of paintings with no brush

I quit smoking my American Spirit Smoky treats for good last week

What-can-I-do-with-my-hands-

What-can-I-do-with-my-hands-

Bop bop bop bop be bop bop bop ba bop bam boom bop be bop bop

ba bop a

Tap ta taptap ta tapity tap tap

Let's have sex. That's funny.

III.

I'll hang out here and wait for you to snap

Again on me

At your slave quarters

Like Hansel follows Gretel on a tight rope

With a handkerchief tied over her child eyes

While my apartment across town rots

And my plants with names die of starvation

And my dishes wont do themselves

##

I'll cook your meals, four courses,

And wait for more of my skin to turn purple

You're older than me, and look like my father looked when I was just

Four.

You take out my trash when you come over,

And you care about the condition of my tires.

##

I'll try to forgive you for what you do.

##

You continue to grow taller than me

Like a rooted vine I planted here in my sleep last year

Until I am

A stump of your landlord's pruned trees hidden underfoot

And you bend down to peel away my bark to see the black underneath

Like your stinger has pumped me full of your color and I am now the

Same

4.

The dark lesion looks like a flag

Faded in sun and wear

The wound you dug

Like a seedling

Into my back

Sewn up, like a branded cow you'd like to save

##

You snap, like a sugary pea in a pod by a pair of hungry fingers

That also plant poisonous orange perennials

For activists to wear in their wavy hair

Bursting through impossible planting areas with invisible seeds

Soiled and thirsty

Your crows feet feed on my earth

Drowning in the dryness of too much sick heat and sunshine

Mirages of pink water cans and middle class mommies and daddies

with common sense

And pleasant advice

Rain and ice and snow and changing of seasons

And music melting under temperature and children playing recorders

To their small pots to keep them growing

5.

My feminism is dead like the fallen leaves of my tiny grocery store

African Violet

It's been shot, by a Nazi Conservative with a cross burning in my yard

I've become a victim of southern warfare and I'm afraid for them to

Win the war

I'm laying in your Bed, clutching a pillow like a Relic with my stubby

Nails

6.

God is in New York, I felt God in New York

Maybe he's in Union square

He's definitely on the G train

Somewhere in the City is a playground of calm and soft strong hands

Love, Art, and clean white sheets

I'm saving up for therapy

I'm saving up for a plane ticket

mermaid salon

i remember us

naked in the bathtub

when i was four

my tiny naked body

wedged between your naked thighs

i remember you washing my hair

as i pretended i was

a mermaid in a salon

at the bottom of the green sea

your red wine is white guitar---sex is from outer space

1

All of the faces look familiar

As I grasp my heavy red suitcase

old and new spirits, some recognizable from something energetically

understood

a mystery, a question, a breath, a meal for the soul

My awkward glances turn to soft butter on the skin of the beautiful

new

Soul brothers and sisters on the strange new subway

The train takes me through the suburbs

My adventure is this life, this city, this intensity

I glance at them with care

As if I have known all of them before

2

the test tube babies weren't formulated to handle

what the world and organized religion and education hands them

our neuro nets are weaving a web in the same direction and the

spoon i fed you with is shiny and new

3

just so you know, that's the only time

i've ever done

anything like that

in a taxicab

you

picture people as rag dolls

meaningless and for your own amusement

dispose of me as you create me as a dispensable being

i know you felt something too

you're human just like me

venerable just like me

used, played like games,

Our bodies overanalyzed

I'm sorry ======I forgot to Photoshop the parts of me

That don't look like Hustler magazine

We are natural beings, the sun, the Son, has born our existence

through

The radiance and power of the philosopher kings' passing spirits

4

Sex is from outer space

We float in pockets, bubbles of matter, ideas in the womb of time,

before birth we sit, chatting, bleeding on each other and

screamingsinginglaughing in silence as we wait for our lips and

tongue

Then in life we find each other-our twins from our alternate

dimension-womb, our soulmates we seek and when we find, we

wonder why we feel so close

Your red wine is a white guitar

The lower east side is an echo of a female voice

Soon to be the man's breath in your ear

With Dirty words

Look on the projector

And you'll See

The breathing-pulsing art of all bodies in one

His film was his soul and it was bloody and spilled on her expensive

shoes

leaving her turned on and ready for what he had next

but left him stripped

Exposed and formulated to be contained, the fire alarm was pulled and a panic arose from the graveyard of Radical Republican peanut

eating soul stealers

He wished he could make a doll

My face With her Lips

Art was dead but resurrection is an alien robot personified

With cookie cutter computer chips for snacks

Hips and buzz

Busy bass

Blasphemy

And the big screen said "yes"

Panoramic Egg

25

unshiny on a bed unmade. crucified upside down. like peter. wearing a black wig with short jagged bangs. faded, buttonless leather, tight. rashy skin. muse. and a dollar tree cross hung crooked on the wall.

21

odor. of industrial waste. and sewer. coupled with the overpowering scent of candied nuts. on the street that made the whole block smell like cake. rush into our brookyln senses. as we get to the city every day. on the blue train. we would stop at 42nd street just to feed our freezing red hungry noses. and feed our lonely minds. with the warmth. of massive crowds. of people. all strange and interesting. shouting and bumping. and cussing. and laughing. and holding too many bags. passing the food stands with the striped umbrellas. breathing it in. as we shoved dry rice cakes. into our purple mouths. on the c train. on our way to our castings in the meatpacking district. buying bruised bananas at the jamaican delis in brookyln on our way home.with our heels in our huge suitcase purses we walk into the lobby and change out of our slimy slushy ug boots and into our heels as people roll their eyes as we walk to the elevator in our black stilettos and look at the list to see what floor our casting is on. we surely wouldn't walk through the city in these heels on the dirty melted snow and ice in february.

22

got some jobs and waiting for checks. the strangers i live with are becoming family. beautiful seesters to name mice with. met some promoters who take us out for food and wine and bottles of champagne we could never afford. were wearing pretty dresses sipping drinks and meeting people, going place to place. And after 5 am we are laughing and tripping over the subway stairs in our crazy heels trying to find our way back to he BK, then going barefoot the rest of the walk home warm with tipsy grins on our baby faces. with my. new sisters. there are so many weird people out after 5 am. and the city makes my adhd feel normal.

22

vomiting metaphors. branded. as heretics like cows. we are creepy dolls with invisible stitches and strings attached we're offered blow before money and we turn it down so were poor

25

broken water pump ancient fridgidare. vampires in trailer parks.
aristocrats vs the artists
can't wash clothes untie dirty corset. go to school

14/6

panoramic egg. i had already. bit the head. off the duck.while you
were asleep. you were angry. you wanted everything. to be perfect
25

you brought me in your white crumpled doggy bag with styrofoam
enclosures.
i wasn't invited. i get your leftovers.
25

american parks. pine needles. Towering. from tree tops like starving
paper airplanes.
hungry for earth and dust and litter. children in mothers SUVS with the
stick figure
stickers. advertising their american dream in a non creative way.
plastic playground
tertiary colors.frowns
25
strings hanging
from ceiling
words blow in a ceiling fan wind current drum circle
like broken ferris wheel motors burning and stinking
on fortune cookie papers

we are grabbing at them

taking turns

with Paper cuts on our pointer fingers

that Open up like portals

deep and full

of blood and Soap

4,5,6

While David Hockney

Slaps my ass

My leopard print pillows are a prayer easily stabbed by dollar store

knives

Feathers flying into the wet paint like tiny windows of the high rise

Our four hands pressed together to form the steeple

My core a vacant church

Your bleeding bones lay at rest at my altar

As five are broken, the rest perfectly structured for awe

We rewrite the Book with our pen names, secret

Your marrow is black ink and my hands guide your pensive cursive

When the lid is kept on the firefly jar

Long after they're dead

My New York Indian Summer

Is yet to repeat itself

As we take communion of whipped cream on laminated porno pins

Wearing rooster caps and the world is a stage for religious

performance art sex

Musicians patting themselves on the back

Pretentious lyrics and baby blue

V necks

Trading in their Polos for the new fad

You play your clever compact discs from the 90's

Roll away the stone

Honest modern art is vagrancy

Hiring fires to burn themselves dry

Planting herb gardens in their empty guitars

After the strings free themselves

From their death sentence

$$

This building houses both gay prostitutes

And daddy's money

In our Book,

We are tearing out Commandments

Until there are only 6 we obey

They switch places like Disney

Running for president, and from the law.

the negative space

bansky's work tiled on the front, i'm glad it's not santa

i hate santa

i feel sorry for santa

...

i open the card he sent

to see a blank inside

on the thick white cardstock

of the seven dollar card

i imagine words with depth that induce an all-encompassing epiphany

about life and love

art, film, music and God

maybe even a marriage proposal

in the negative space you tell me of your love

how much you have grown to understand the power of man made

time and the universe

you see us as street art hippies married by the paint that covers our

bodies,

we spray paint our way to peace, believing in all the Gods

the myths

the prophecies about 2012 as we live as if the black hole will eat us

up

as your darkness actualizes from your 6 ft support

off of the canvas and into the center of the earth, eating

our free spirited love festin' asses for lunch

and we are holding hands like it's a fucking carnival

spinning like faceted smoky quartz on a wire

all of the tangible is crushed as the planet collapses upon space and

all you cared about was our art

as 2012 approaches

the month of december we would dread for a new reason,

not just because it has become a consumer holiday month that makes

us feel like bad friends because we don't have enough money to buy

our way to love for this misconstrued

now commercialized holiday time

we set the alarms on our clocks

and clean out our pantries

all we have lived for was love and when the world collapses, in black

our expired processed food thrown into the streets

ideologies actualized into tangible human forms,

disguised as 3 kings, the size of giants

trampling the boxes, the dry grains and mold

under their ancient brandless sandals

as humanity has come back to claim back humanity

chemically separating this last judgement as a prophecy of candy and

carnivals,

creepy and archaic

trying to scientifically make sense of this metaphor that has been

tried and tired like an old prostitute

inducing our experimental waking lucid dream

on the cheap grits ground government commissioned asphalt

as we have saved and worked

our entire humble lives for what for some has carelessly been

destroyed,

we have not let this technologically driven trojan virus breeding

conspiracy laden aspect of the media,

an army of 4 billion without arms or legs, a Photoshopped nation of

lies and self hatred

make us hate ourselves for not looking perfect and maintaining that

image

we are imperfect and silly, ridiculous and artistic, married by the fact

that we are too ridiculous for anyone else

i close the blank daydream card, and realize i'm more likely to

become a nun.

Coming of Age-The Bullet

Rummaging through the junk I hoard for stupid sentimental reasons

In the top drawer, cluttered with memorabilia that would be better off forgotten

I am remembering why I am weird

And searching for truth

About who I am

Leafing through my makeshift books I used to write as a child

Pictures drawn with faded markers and words carefully written in a child's confident scribble

On computer paper, stapled together or pages tied together through unevenly punched holes

Tied together with worn purple yarn

Words simple and loaded

Free spirited illustrations not tainted by critics or instruction

Pouring the contents of an old vitamin bottle found in the drawer

From the 1980's

Coins from Thailand. France.

I sift through the grouping of smooth metal discs

And My forgotten Civil War bullet is left alone in my hand, coins
pouring onto the floor

Holding the cold finding in my palm, heavy for its size

Tan coating chipped to reveal dull silver underneath

I imagine you once filled with wonder

Rolling the bullet in your palm

Like I am

Feeling the heaviness on your skin

An artifact, like an Egyptian charm bracelet- tarnished and dirty

As a child it would fascinate me to know

This was part of a larger picture, connecting me to the storybook-like

happenings in my textbooks

Like death and war

I am at war with myself

The men I have chosen have beat me, raped me, ran around on me

I'd blame myself, or anyone I could

I used to blame you, I'd tell myself

That you could have taught me what to watch out for, the red flags

How to stand up for myself back then

But I know now that you're not to blame

I was stupid, impulsive, had to learn the hard way

When I was only 16

And you wanted the best for me, you didn't know how to save me, I was wild

You have given me a bullet with no gun

And coins for countries I could never afford to travel to

I am empty now like the dusty open bottle,

And you are as foreign to me as the coins

Eventually I will know you, each day I know and love you more

As you become more open and free as you age, it gives me life

I'm saving up for a plane ticket, and one day I will use these Coins

I'll send everyone postcards, I may never come home

TETRAMORPHS TANGLED IN OUR CURLS

absidial chapels as hideouts

the burgundy dresses with windy bottoms walking by themselves on

invisible women exiting the safehouses, cloth folded in prayer, blowing

in slow motion to the beat of the light "ting" of the child's toy triangle

choreographed like a pretentious perfection imposed upon our senses

by an artistic film that seethes with blasphemy, brainwashing us with

its enticing self-indulgent and self-proclaimed profound statements

that propose to save our souls with redundant dry messages,

regurgitated by corporate assfucks as we are eaten by the gigantic

fried chickens we once consumed, giggling in the belly of the whales,

gurgling, we taste our sauces as we swim in them

the expensive cinematography stabs us to death in our consummate

demise

the sound track is ridiculous, deep and airy

as Jeff Buckley is singing covers of our death cab for cutie cd-

he was resurrected from the 90's dead, ditched his cliche flannel

getup and coolguy bicycle

a new and improved rotted body of musical bliss

with an emo haircut and trendy tattoos, skinny jeans and rider boots

he jumps in– to the consumer nation to become a product of the 21st
century

his beautiful lips a corpse of something nostalgic and deathly sick

like a stomach acid lollipop of overconsumption and self loathing

as the sun explodes, harlem is rained on by bridges of fire for
volcanos to cross

TETRAMORPHS take flight into our

expensive haircuts

the beauty of the beasts-

tangling themselves in our tightly sprayed curls

phenomenology inscribed on our backs and palms

as the government thinks of ways to plant ID chips into out arms in
shots

to poison our blood stream

as we laugh because the schizophrenics were right all along!

the masked man, dressed in skin with a black mandala

acting as a judge, with Jesus in his cage

giving the sign of Benediction with his left hand and left toes

guns on his right and the saved to his left

his limp body is a construction of our beings, for what flesh of ours he

could not eat he dressed himself in, taking our hands and feet and

beings as his to consume

not knowing that our beings glow as Relics, as we rise together as

one, skins combined to consume his evil, we have the power as

de-frag-men-ted beings as a blind eyeless earless Groupthink

as he sheds his coat of Us

throwing us, casting us, onto the streets of Bedsty

dead archangels graffiti the street with their heavenly bodies

as self expression born out of the womb of morbidity sparked by the

mind controlling commercial GI track- deviation of humanity

rises up as a Black man is president, we are dawning a new age for

the people who once had no hope,

creative people, minorities, women, black men

we are all bound together by the common threads of a suppressive

society

creating a quilt that covers the eyes and binds the hands of the

corrupt governmental schemes to keep us down, we tie up the man with our happy metaphorical renderings and new found unity

snakes bite our breasts as sex before marriage is cheap and sold

online

i paint the memory of his living breathing eyes and body onto my

canvas

his dark soul shines as a black figure, someone i love, someone i cant

penetrate with my unbridled selflessness as i learn selfishness as a

defense mechanism

i cover him with pink and red, my brush dips the liquitex, heavy body,

cadmium beautiful

buried artistically for a death in my mind heavily represented by my

representation on my drawing board, 30 by 40, prestretched snow

white canvas covered in the blood of my new found happiness, death

is a rebirth and not something that is a literal death but the death of

old beliefs and empty lifestyle

buried for my art

i cover his head in green, for i painted him there not to gaze at him

but to change him in my world, my created world

his pasted body becomes a flower, the red and pink become the petals and the green the stem, my brush rests in the murky water, a

color of its own

the color of my blood will bleed the color of mixed paint and water

but it is not my time

my uterus

is hungry for children, not politics

but mostly

starving for solid spiritual sustenance

not satisfied by anything other than

the seeking

of Him/Her/Intelligent energy/God that sustains the universe

glitter bath

the collaged sketchbook leaks rubbing alcohol

to sterilize the petty truths told and the fingers bleeding from the
paper cuts

words with sharp edges

storms inside these pages

smear ink and faces and old words

the blood sluiced by the pouring cloud

smearing blue and black on your thin fingers

as you bend and stretch and throw ball

preparing yourself to beat your wall into submission

covering up all your shameful truths with purple,

the color of bruises and the color of my bedspread

*

today I dyed my hair black and tied a piece of black lace three times around my left wrist

because black means go

i hide in my studio to mourn first the loss of the artist

and second the death of the tall stack of white painted bricks built to become a living breathing being

taking in sun and making its own food

bringing together black and white with yellow ladders and lesbians and straights

in the free world the tables are full of breads and teas and fruits made to share

as we eat we rescue the bones from the animals and put them in our hair, red and blonde and black

and before sleep we shower in baths of glue to lay down to rest in beds of loose glitter

antelope arches

outside, as if for the first time,

feeling the grounding of my gravity

 on the green velvet ground

under arches of confused and tired time travel feet

will transport my grace from its hiding joke-world

as i'm watching my mother have her C section and i'm the one inside

each day, rebirth, scissors and glue,

gold foil, paper dolls

torn where once held hands

how to fix

being broken

stitch it up

wear the scar

each tiny noise and movement of alive

comes from an intelligent composer, directed by time

my father has come into his own, saved me from myself with

warm dinners and sincere hugs

words of love i have waited for my whole life

everything in the past that was lacking has come all at once

and i am full, and thankful, and living a new life

time is running out for us as we live in bliss that

is far from sheltered or ignorant as each creature

feels, knows, and

earth welcomes our footsteps as we destroy

and create with love and hate. its art

music of nature

filling our ears with truth and age

spiral staircases of black widows weave webs for cycles

harpooning our whales with our war-stained antelope arches

veins

wake with intentions iced like confetti

lincoln log confidence

build mazes for rodents

brutally pry open the closed with a scraper

where rooftops are colored with plastic insides

rush to understand what we cant in our death

when beautiful colored hillsides and fresh earthy markets

where farmers display their humble wares for the crowd

and their souls are rooted deep in the country with

fields that flow deeper and farther with veins

are replaced with sick purgatory candelabras

with heavy white wax

that sticks to our fingers

and crusts up our hair

like icicle torments

that pray for distraction

in life, and death (the bus ride with the open window)

i can feel myself smiling

see myself glow

actualizing

head titled hair wild

my rich brown skin, wild woman

like a camera watching myself

out of body below

lips open and wide into clean rushing wind

natural hair like climbing vines crawling forward and around

teeth-creme colored reflection-for invisible eyes

skin burnt clean by dry upstate air

senses feel deeply elements colliding with skin

feel - against chipped passing houses of pain and discovery

where my tiny head slept

lullabies, screaming and yelling

chaos nursing sleep

this river, grey sky portal

this town

broken down, beautiful grave

dried flood of destruction and help

this place that i love

that corrected my ignorance

frosted glass and curiosity

created some cynical child of mine to mime

i'll never get out and plant feet on twisted earth

i'll just pass, keep on riding, wild

i can see myself laughing

white teeth to the blue sky mimicking clouds

head lifts higher and higher, hair tangling on whatever is around

i can look at this place, or close my eyes and feel it

and wherever i go i know i have arrived

strength inside, memories dead

ghost of child runs through grass and waves to me goodbye, or

maybe hello

love.

www.ingramcontent.com/pod-product-compliance
Lightning Source LLC
Chambersburg PA
CBHW060040040426
42331CB00032B/1835